BEGIN
WITHIN

Rev. Sunshine Daye

BEGIN WITHIN

A Playbook for Living Your Genuine Life

Sunshine Daye

2014

Copyright © 2014 Revered Sunshine Daye
All Rights Reserved
Published in the United States by Create Space, an Amazon company.
www.createspace.com ~ www.amazon.com

CREATE SPACE logo design is a registered trademark of this Amazon company.

ISBN-13: 978-1500451660

Printed in the United States of America

Design by Caitlin Crest ~ www.ZephyrGraphics.com
Cover by Shauna McNamara - www.sdesignmedia.com

This playbook is dedicated to the
revealing of the great I AM that is all of us.

Welcome!

It is my joy to present this book to the world. The things I write about in the following pages are near and dear to me, as this practice has helped me live a rich, fulfilling life.

The purpose of this guide is to help establish and incorporate principles and practices in life that will help you succeed in your endeavors. It takes consistent repetition and action to develop a belief. Keep new steps small and increase them slowly and steadily until you reach your intended goal. As this becomes your daily practice your life will begin to change in noticeable ways.

Focus on the topic of your choice daily for an entire month. Each topic contains a definition, an affirmation, an inspirational message, a spiritual mind treatment, a journaling opportunity and a time of stillness and silence. By keeping your focus on one topic every day for an entire month, you begin to incorporate new thoughts and ideas as a way of life. These thoughts become a habit and these habits become your beliefs. Our behaviors are based on our beliefs. For example, I believe that when I lift the switch on the wall, the light bulb will light up a darkened room. So, without thinking about it (auto-pilot), when I want light, I get up from whatever I am doing, walk over to the switch and lift it. In the same way, when I believe that my life is abundant and a situation arises where an unexpected bill or expense comes my way, my behavior (auto-pilot) demonstrates that my life is abundant because I simply look for all the avenues I have to pay for it! This and so much more will come to pass for you too, once you incorporate this way of thinking and being.

This book contains writings and maps of the "life" plays that lead you to successful living. The following pages contain directions on how to use this playbook to achieve maximum results. I call this the Begin Within Playbook because it holds the strategies, plans and tactics needed to achieve a winning life free from all discord.

Set your intention and dedicate at least five minutes to this daily practice. The more time you devote to yourself and your inner growth, the more realizations and insights you will have. You will undergo vital changes and develop a more powerful sense of self. You will become conscious of how powerful, how beautiful, and how loving you are, and you will experience success in your life. Celebrate the small successes and acknowledge your areas of growth more than you criticize yourself for not doing something. If it takes weeks or months, celebrate what you do!

Set an alarm for a certain time like it is an appointment you can't miss. Having a specific time of day or night and having it follow a specific activity will ensure success in your daily practice.

It is my intention to guide and support you through the experiential process of remembering, embracing and knowing who you really are. May you achieve and experience peace and success in life.

You are Life Itself! Agape,

Sunshine Daye

Trim this page on the dotted line. It's a bookmark to keep your place as you read. →

I'm Here!

"Your vision will become clear only when you can look into your heart. Who looks outside, dreams: who looks inside, awakens."

Carl Jung

Begin Within
Rev. Sunshine Daye

I'm Here!

*"From within
I let my heart begin
to see eternity.
Turn within
and now
I can begin
to see the
face of God.
Face of God
is all I am and
face of God
is all I see.
Ever present,
all around me.
It's within me.
It's within!"*
Rickie Byars Beckwith

Begin Within
Rev. Sunshine Daye

Table of Contents

Essential Instructions	10
The Use of Definitions	11
The Use of Quotes	11
The Use of the Inspirational Message	11
The Use of Spiritual Mind Treatment	12
The Use of Affirmation	14
The Use of Stillness and Silence	16
The Use of Journal Writing	18

Monthly Themes:

Abundance	19
Beauty	23
Beginning	27
Bliss/Joy	31
Clarity	35
Connectedness	39
Faith	43
Imagine	47
Peace	51
Purpose	55
Thankfulness	59
Wholeness	63
Worthiness	67

Let's Begin Within

Essential Instructions

Be gentle with yourself as you begin this process. Review the instructions and start at your own level of comfort.

Look at the Table of Contents and decide which theme you would like to incorporate in your life over the next 30 days.

Turn to that topic and place your bookmark there.

Each day, for the entire month read the quotes and definition silently and then read the spiritual mind treatment and affirmation aloud.

Enter into a time of stillness and silence, keeping in mind what you have read.

Enjoy the moments and engage in writing your immediate thoughts in your journal or write down your experiences throughout the day. Many people write down specific insights from their time in the stillness and silence. The choice is yours whether or not you write in a journal. Many folks find it helpful and uplifting to release their thoughts on paper.

If you are new to the practice of a time of stillness and silence, you can begin using five minute increments each week. Be gentle with yourself.

Begin by reading the same monthly theme every day – each theme consists of the quotes, definition, inspirational message, spiritual mind treatment and affirmations. Then enter a time of stillness and silence and/or journal writing. Remember, you are developing a way of being and this is the beginning of a daily practice that will enhance, uplift and advance your life to its personal greatness.

Each week increase your time of stillness and silence by five minutes. For example;

Week 1
Every day read the monthly theme then enter a time of stillness and silence for at least five minutes

Week 2
Every day read the monthly theme then enter a time of stillness and silence for at least ten minutes

Week 3
Every day read the monthly theme then, enter a time of stillness and silence for at least 15 minutes

Week 4+
Every day read the monthly theme then enter a time of stillness and silence for at least 20 minutes

Option 2

You have the option of adding an additional five minutes of journaling each day to any of the above scenarios.

The Use of Definition

Each monthly topic and theme has a definition. The definition gives meaning to the word, and direction and focus for the month. It is often said "words don't have meaning, people give them meaning." Based on this quote, ask yourself, does the word have the same meaning to you as the definition given? What does it mean to you? How does the meaning of the word expand or refine?

This is your book, so add your own definitions and nuances by writing in the blank spaces or in the margins. Your daily practice of reading the definition silently helps incorporate the meaning of the words and also deepens their meanings for you. As the days go by the definition and meaning may expand and incorporate other ideas; feel free to write them down in the pages of this book or in your journal.

The Use of Quotes

Each monthly theme will have at least two quotes. Read each quote slowly, seeking to understand the writer's message. Allow yourself to become open to the message for you.

If a related quote comes to mind, please write that quote in your book. Use your quote and the quotes available to anchor the topic for the month.

The Use of the Inspirational Message

Read the inspirational message to yourself out loud or silently. Notice what stands out for you, what resonates with you and what comes up for you? What message is being relayed? Is this something that you can accept fully now? Are you willing to know the message firsthand for yourself?

The Use of this Playbook

You will notice large open spaces throughout this Playbook! They are intentional and presented for your playful pleasure. Use them to make notes, doodle, jot, and keep track of your inner alchemy as you move through the process of change and empowerment that Begins Within!

The Use of Spiritual Mind Treatment

One of the most important ways to *Begin Within* is Spiritual Mind Treatment. Treatments are also known as affirmative prayer, used to state Truth and anchor in our own awareness that which is true of all life, especially your life. Developed by Dr. Ernest Holmes, founder of Religious Science and author of *The Science of Mind* as well as many other metaphysical works, this type of prayer is used by thousands of people around the world daily. There is a scientific reasoning underlying all prayer. Through this process of reasoning we are treating our own mind about the subject of our prayer.

Prayer does nothing to God. Prayer brings the one praying to an awareness of God, an understanding that all is well. This consciousness in itself does the healing. The power of prayer has been known since the beginning of time. Each of us has found our own ways to experience and express our connection to that Life which is greater than our daily events and challenges. Spiritual Mind Treatment is one of the many ways people pray. As you use this form of prayer you will find it effective and uplifting.

Here is a short list of the attributes of God – Omniscience, Omnipotence, Omnipresence, Immutable, Love, Joy, Peace, Power, Creative, Abundance, Harmony, Wisdom, Beauty, Balance, Freedom, Wholeness, Clarity,

Prayer Treatment uses five steps. Here is the explanation and purpose of each step.

Step 1 - Recognition

Begin by recognizing that "God is all," including the issue of the prayer. Name as many attributes of God you can think of to begin "treating your mind" toward the idea that there is a power greater than you are, and greater than the issue at hand. Remember, you are not making God these things; you are reminding yourself that this is what God is. There is only God and there is nothing else. This step is often compared to meditation.

Use whatever name is comfortable for you for God - Spirit, Life, Infinite Intelligence, Mother Earth, Father Sky, Divine Love, Total Peace. I will often use God or Life in the examples.

> **SAMPLE**: *There is one life - that life is God. God/It/Life is always the same. It is timeless, changeless, everywhere present, all powerful, and all knowing. God is love, abundance, beauty, creativity, divine order, freedom, harmony, joy, eternal life, peace, power, wholeness, wisdom and oneness. God is All and God created everything out of Itself. God is omnipresence, omniscience and omnipotence! I believe in God, only God and nothing else!*

Step 2 - Unification

It may be easy to state that God is all these things. It may be difficult to identify yourself with these same attributes. However, it is essential to know your life is really the Life of God made manifest in the flesh and that which is true of God is true of you, since you are the way God expresses in form. You are "made in the image and likeness of God." You can only be the magnificence, abundance, beauty, creativity, power, and love that God is. All that you have just declared God to be is what you are and all you will ever be! This step is also compared to meditation because it is used to ponder and to deepen our understanding.

> **SAMPLE**: *God is All and God created everything out of Itself. Therefore my life is that very life that God is. I am an unrepeatable expression of Life. God and I are one; therefore that which is true of God is true of me since I am of God, one with God, living and being in God; God living and being in me! The love that God is I am. The peace that God is I am. God is expressing through me, as me, in each moment, now and forevermore. All that I am is expressing Life/God!*

Step 3 - Realization

The third step is a declaration of the truth stated above. It is always worded in the first person and in the present tense. You are not asking, begging or pleading for anything. You are declaring and affirming that it is the Truth and it's a done deal. You are recognizing that this is your Truth now. Accept that it can be nothing other than the Truth.

Remember, you are adjusting your own mind and you are doing that by clearly stating the Truth of God and the truth about yourself. If you are praying for someone else you use his or her name where yours would be.

> **SAMPLE**: *I speak this word for myself knowing that everything is coming together for my good. I now accept the Truth of my being. I know Divine right action is active in my life now. I experience the wholeness, joy and love in all areas of life. I experience wholeness in my health, relationships, and finances. I am abundant and all my needs are met with enough to spare and share. My accounts and friends are plentiful. My mind and body experiences health and wholeness, as every organ, action and function follows the divine pattern of eternal life.*

The Truth of God is the Truth of my life. I easily and effortlessly know my greatest good, know it is my Divine gift and the Truth of my being. I am always in the right place at the right time. The Wisdom of God within me guides my every move. I experience unconditional love flowing through me at all times. I feel the perfection of God in every cell of my body. I am total harmony and joy in every area of my life. I see God in every situation in my life.

Step 4 - Thanksgiving

Step four gives you an opportunity to express thanks for the Truth that you have come to know and realize and for its triumphant completion. It follows the statement "pray believing that it is done" – when I pray believing it is done I naturally enter a phase of thanksgiving. When someone opens a door I give thanks for the kindness – likewise when I believe it is done then I am grateful and thankful. Notice I have used grateful, thankful, giving thanks, and showing my gratitude, etc. Each statement has a nuance that differentiates one from the other. Use the one that resonates with you the most and use the others at your pleasure. The purpose of this step is to arrive at the feeling tone that it is already done, so you give thanks and begin to see all the ways it is already your Truth.

> **SAMPLE**: *I give thanks for the knowing of this Truth. I am grateful that this word is already made manifest in the mind of God and I joyfully expect its demonstration as my experience. Filled with thanksgiving for the spiritual Law which responds to my word, I am confident that my good is already unfolding through me now.*

Step 5 - Release

It's time to release this prayer. The work is already done in your mind and now it is time to demonstrate that you now know the Law will do its work - through you. This is known as letting go and letting Life "do what it do!"

> **SAMPLE**: *I release this prayer to the Law. I know it is done so I allow it to be made manifest now as I joyfully allow it to be so. And so it is!*

The Use of Affirmations

"The greatest discovery of my generation is that human beings can alter their lives by altering their attitudes of mind."
~ William James

Great affirmations are present tense, powerful, personal and positive. When working with affirmations it is best to say them aloud several times, clearly, and distinctly. This activity creates the habit of affirming your good, begins to fill the content of your consciousness with Truth and activates parts of your brain that hear the information, process it, and store it for later use. Your affirmations give shape and direction to your thought. Your feelings and sensations are part of the creative process, so the more feeling you feel with your affirmations the greater the power you have over conditions.

Affirmations are NOT:

- A plea to some outside source to grant you what you are affirming
- A magic trick on your mind
- A quick fix
- A stand-alone answer

Affirmations are used by professionals, spiritual people, athletes, children and ordinary people in every day in life. Ever notice when someone gives you a compliment? It's an affirmation. When people criticize you or others this is also a form of affirmation. Negative affirmations are not great, yet they may lead us to an awakening that is necessary. Your self-chatter is also an affirmation. The daily practice in *Begin Within* supports you in saying your affirmations aloud to help reduce the degrading mind chatter and increase the powerful, affirmative, positive internal dialogue that will help you achieve and out picture your greatness.

When we begin this practice of affirming our Truth, we are making a deposit into our spiritual bank account. We are, indeed, building ourselves up so that we can know our Truth, experience success, and live from our natural place of wholeness, peace, power, love, joy, abundance and harmony.

So remember, make sure your affirmations begin with "I am or I can" or "my life is." Make them bold, powerful and believable, say them aloud to yourself several times a day, commit to the process even when you feel uncomfortable and work through the discomfort. You can do it! Within you is all of Life and its greatness. You can surely tap into that greatness when you *Begin Within*. Take action, keep up your daily practices and keep affirming your Truth.

Each monthly subject has an affirmation page created with a beautiful photo to accompany it, so that you may cut it out of the playbook and hang it up somewhere so you will be reminded of your affirmation throughout each day of the month.

Write

Your

Favorite

Affirmations

Here

The Use of a Time of Stillness and Silence

Having some time of stillness and silence is important for the incorporation of new ideas and a new way of life. We can use our time of stillness and silence in many different ways.

Try the practice of meditation. Meditation is simply a time of stillness and silence with a purpose. There are many kinds of meditation so I will give you a few ideas as to how to utilize your time of stillness and silence most effectively. You are encouraged to try these and other forms of meditation available.

Stillness and Silence
Free Flow Meditation

This meditative practice is simply allowing your mind to rest in the spaces between the thoughts. For those who are new to meditation, here are some guidelines: Get in a comfortable position, in a chair or on the floor, use a pillow or mat if you'd like to, gently close your eyes or leave them open, but be still. Breathe naturally. Notice the air as it enters your nose. Put your attention there. Count your breaths up to four and backwards down to one. If you lose your place, start back at one. Gently use your breath as the focus until it just is. You may hear noises, sounds, or movement around you. Accept it. It is a confirmation of your life, be joy-filled about it and tenderly bring your attention back to your breath. Have the stillness and the silence be internal, in your mind and body.

At first, it may be helpful to set a gentle audible timer for five, ten, 15 or 20 minutes so you are not concerned with time. You do not have to use a timer, it is completely up to you.

The key of time in the stillness and silence is to make it a regular daily practice so that you are anchoring the Truth of your being and dedicating time for your own spiritual well-being. During this practice you may discover a song inside of you, an answer, an invention, or a way of being that sets you free from all discord.

Contemplative Meditation
Focused Meditation

The purpose of contemplative meditation is to focus your thinking mind on the mysteries of being or on recognizing the interdependence and oneness of life. When you use contemplative meditation first read a passage, and then seek to know the answer to one of the following questions; what does the writer mean by this? What is the intention of the writer? In what ways does this fit into my life? What does this mean to me and in what ways can I effectively use and incorporate it into my life? What is yearning to be birthed?

Select a comfortable posture and quiet place for meditation. Examine your body and relax any tension. Notice the cadence of your breath, feel the rise and fall of your inhale and your exhale. Let your attention gently land on your breath and begin to make use of an introspective question. What does this mean to me and in what ways can I effectively utilize and incorporate this in my life? What is breathing me? Contemplate the source of your breath. Consider the many ways life is for you and know that all creation is in rhythm of the same breath.

If you have used a timer, when it alerts you, take an additional recess to evoke a sense of gratitude and celebration for your dedication and soak up the energetic vibration produced in the silence. If you have no time constraints, simply be with the stillness until you feel the gentle end of your meditation.

Once your contemplative meditation is complete, you can happily re-emerge into your day. Some people use journal writing as a tool to slowly emerge into their day. Whether you journal or simply re-emerge with a smile, use whatever method feels best to you.

Mantra Meditation
Affirmation Meditation

Mantras are phrases or words chanted during meditation to call forth our spiritual Truth. The sounds become the focus. In this form of meditation you can use your mantras or affirmations silently, quietly or out loud during your meditation time. The mantra *Om* is often used since it delivers a deep vibration that makes it easy for the mind to concentrate on that particular sound.

According to Deepak Chopra, a New Age Guru, the word Mantra means "instrument of the mind." A mantra takes us to the source of the mind, which is spirit. Mantras are powerful intentions, subtle in nature that stimulate the vibratory field that leads us to our innate Truth.

Some people use a *Mala (prayer beads) to count mantras. Mantras are also known as Sanskrit prayers. Sanskrit prayers are done in sets of 108 repetitions. You may use affirmations or a mantra by repeating phrases or words while gently holding a bead in your hand. This deliberate action permits us to experience the transformation of our consciousness. It stimulates healing and the fulfillment of our desires through the vibratory arena of creation. Keep your mind focused on your mantra, let go, and repeat it slowly.

108 resonates with me in this way:

1 = One Power, One Presence, and One Life.
0 = Emptiness or completeness of our spiritual practice - to be so empty or so full is a beautiful quality.
8 = Eternal and infinite nature of Life.

We may use this practice to know the One Life so completely that we are empty of desire because we are fulfilled now and forevermore.

*Visit www.sunshinedaye.com to see the beautiful Malas that Sunshine creates.

The Use of Journal Writing

The value of using a personal journal for enhancing your growth and learning is immense. Journal writing helps promote inner reflection. It's a canvas to paint with words what's going on inside your own thoughts, emotions, consciousness, and feelings.

Journal writing helps you examine your feelings in a way that is not threatening to anyone. You can look at what you think and feel about a particular topic, examine your spiritual progress, and develop and incorporate new thoughts and ideas for healing and personal spiritual growth.

Journal writing can also help instill affirmations, as well as let you blow off a little steam, by letting go of ideas, thoughts and feelings that no longer resonate with your new insights. Who knows, journaling might even lead you to some phenomenal idea to solve a problem, a dilemma or situation that is baffling you. As with anything new, the more you do it the easier it flows.

Prompt Questions for journaling:

- What does the monthly theme mean to me?
- In what ways does the inspirational message move me to action? If so describe the action
- What can I discover about myself, my situation, and/or life?
- What is different about me today than when I started this process?
- What did I learn today? In what ways does it apply to me?
- What affirmations are emerging through me?
- What conversations do I get to have today? Who is involved?
- Was I hurt today? Did I hurt anyone with my words or actions today?
- What must I focus on today?
- What were my dreams last night?
- What do I desire to manifest today?
- What will/did I notice today? Who will/did I notice today?
- What will I express today? In what ways?
- How am I showing up in my life with this new information?

Abundance

Today I recognize my abundance.
I am abundant. I live in an abundant world.
All my needs are met. An abundance of money flows to me.
An abundance of beauty, love, creativity and joy surround me.
Right where I am abundance is and I experience it fully.
I allow and accept
                    my abundance to flow in,
                                  through, and as my life.

Rev. Sunshine Daye

Cut out this page and hang it in your bedroom, office, bathroom, kitchen, or anywhere else you will have the opportunity to read it daily. With love, from Sunshine ♥

Abundance

We are surrounded by abundance even when it does not seem so. When you adopt Abundance as your focus for this month you will develop a keen sense of how abundant your life really is. This month, your daily practice enlarges upon your current concept of abundance.

Definition
Ample, quantity, plentiful, more than adequate amounts.

Quotes
"We see abundance in the Universe. We cannot count the grains of sand on a single beach. The earth contains untold riches, and the very air is vibrant with power." ~ Ernest Holmes

"Doing what you love is the cornerstone of having abundance in your life." ~ Wayne Dyer

Inspirational Message
Expect abundance every day! Abundance is a frame of mind. Take a look around and see the abundance of life. Even in the most challenging circumstances, like being on a freeway caught in traffic, see the abundance of cars and people on that one road. You cannot deny abundance there, can you?

Be ready to experience the abundance of your life. Doing what you love is an example of living an abundant life. There are so many ways your life is abundant. Think about it! When you go out to dinner with friends your life is abundant. Abundance showed up as friends, rich conversation, and money to pay for dinner, a place to go and a way to get there. When someone treats you to a movie or a ball game or a cup of coffee recognize your abundance.

Ask yourself, in what activities am I participating? Is abundance only about money for me? In what ways besides finances do I experience my abundance? The answers to these questions are important for you to know.

Becoming aware of your attitudes and beliefs about abundance makes a huge difference in your ability to accept good. Lose the idea that to be spiritual you must be poor. Drop the thought that money is the root of all evil and dismiss the notion that only greedy people are rich. Embrace the fact that you are abundant. Take on the persona of one who lives richly. See yourself generous with your time, money and energy.

Begin within each day, knowing that Life is conspiring for your good. Live from a knowing that there is good in the world and you ought to have it!

Spiritual Mind Treatment on Abundance
I believe in God – the Divine Creative Intelligence of all, the One Power, One Presence, One Life, all knowing, everywhere present and all powerful. God is all there is. God is Abundance, Infinite, Indivisible, Absolute, Beauty, Peace and Love! God created everything, therefore my life is the life of God. God expresses as me, as the trees, mountains, sun, sky, as everything, for God is everything. I speak this word now for and about the Abundance I am.

I experience abundance in all areas of my life. Abundant Joy, Peace, Love, Creativity flow through and as me now. I see the abundance in my life and in the lives of others. There is enough and plenty to flow to all, in all ways. I embrace abundance as my natural state. I increase my idea of abundance now, accepting that all has been given and to the degree that I know and accept my good I experience it. I am wealthy, healthy and wise. Abundance abounds. My spiritual, mental and financial accounts flourish and overflow abundantly. I have plenty to share and I give freely from a space of plentitude. I am abundant. Plenty flows to me and through me as I participate in the flow of life. I am now open and receptive to the unlimited Source that is my life.

I give thanks abundantly for knowing this Truth and for all the ways I am already abundant. With gratitude I accept my good. I release this Truth into the Law of God. I joyfully look forward to experiencing abundance demonstrating in my Life. And so it is!

Affirmation

Today I recognize my abundance. I am abundant. I live in an abundant world. All my needs are met. An abundance of money flows to me. An abundance of beauty, love, creativity and joy surround me. Right where I am abundance is and I experience it fully. I allow and accept my abundance to flow in, through, and as my life.

Stillness and Silence, and Journal Writing

Enter a time of stillness and silence. Spend some time free flow writing about Abundance or use the prompt questions on page 18.

Beauty

The beauty that I seek is within me.
Beauty is all around me.
I express myself in beauty filled ways.
I get to see the beauty in others.
In life, all things are beautiful,
and it is a joy recognizing that beauty.

Cut out this page and hang it in your bedroom, office, bathroom, kitchen, or anywhere else you will have the opportunity to read it daily. The best beauty product is a smile. ♥ Sunshine

Beauty

We are encircled by beauty even when it does not seem so. When you use Beauty as your motivation for this month you will develop a strong sense of how your life is filled with beauty. This month, your daily practice broadens your current concept of beauty.

Definition
A combination of internal, external and physical qualities that pleases the senses; for example – aesthetic, shape, color, or form, especially but not limited to the sight sense.

Quotes
"Beauty is not in the face; beauty is a light in the heart." ~ Kahlil Gibran

"At some point you have to own up to how great you are, how beautiful you are, to how much inner dignity and potential you have. Drop complaining about what other people didn't give you or do for you, or how they mistreated you. Take repossession of your Self, and you will rise to a level of greatness that has been yours all along." ~ Michael Bernard Beckwith

Inspirational Message
Take a moment to recognize your own beauty, and the beauty around you. Become open to the idea that inner beauty and physical beauty vary from person to person. Have you developed your own sense of what is beautiful to you or are you using what the world labels as beauty by default? Beauty is neither masculine nor feminine – beauty simply is! Beauty is found in all aspects of life.

Remember that you are full of beauty and thus, beautiful. There are no mistakes in creation. The size and shape of your lips, the texture of your hair, the width of your nose, the color of your skin, your height and body type are all patterned by beauty. You were born exactly as you are to display the beauty of all life! There is beauty in what we may think or perceive to be a mistake. As you begin to appreciate and value who you are you will recognize the gift that you are to the world. Become grateful for the beauty within you. You are eternally demonstrating an unrepeatable beauty that is you!

When you begin to fully express your life as beauty, the world around you will mirror back that beauty. Your inner qualities shine so brightly that it is easy for others to see your beauty, feel your beauty and appreciate your beauty. Do not hide your light under a bushel.

Begin within each day, recognizing your own beauty, and then recognize the beauty that surrounds you in nature. Begin within each day, believing you live in a beautiful world and your beauty is a contributing factor to the universal beauty that is!

Spiritual Mind Treatment on Beauty
All I need to know is God. God is all knowing, everywhere present and all powerful. God Is Beauty, Peace and Love! There is no otherness. There is Only God. God made everything out of Itself, therefore I am Beauty, Peace and Love. God is simply expressing beautifully in human form as me. That which is true of God is true of me since nothing separates me from the One.

This One Life is What I Am! This Life is Beauty. Beauty is mine now!

I see and experience my inner and outer beauty. Beauty is all around me and I choose that which is for my highest and best. My life is surrounded and filled with beauty. The splendor of life is plentiful. All that is lovely expresses freely as my gifts and talents.

Magnificence flows to me and through me as I participate in the stream of life. I am now open and receptive to experience unlimited beauty. When things may not automatically appear or seem beautiful, I pause and search for the ways beauty appears, in that situation, circumstance and/or experience. With ease I set aside judgment and seek beauty instead.

I give thanks for knowing Divine Beauty as my Truth. Beauty is the Truth of all life. I Release this into the Law of God. I joyfully look forward to beauty demonstrating in my Life. And so it is!

Affirmation

The beauty that I seek is within me. Beauty is all around me. I express myself in beauty filled ways. I get to see the beauty in others. In life, all things are beautiful and it is a joy recognizing all the beauty that surrounds me.

Stillness and Silence, and Journal Writing

Enter a time of stillness and silence. Spend some time free flow writing about Beauty or use the prompt questions on page 18.

Today is a new day and my new beginning.

On this day I am commencing a beneficial life and
a new way of being in the world.

I am love.

I am kind to all who cross my path today,
by speaking an inspiring word, sharing a smile,
or being a good listener.
Today, I expect a miracle,
and today I am beginning a successful life
of health, wealth and spiritual progress.

I am open-minded and willing to begin.

Beginning

Rev. Sunshine Daye

Cut out this page and hang it in your bedroom, office, bathroom, kitchen, or anywhere else you will have the opportunity to read it daily. Every new beginning comes from some other beginning's end. ♥ Sunshine

Beginning

We are beginning all the time - even when it does not seem so. When you use Beginning as your stimulus for this month you will grow in understanding of the splendor of starting anew. This month, your daily practice expands upon your existing perception of beginning.

Definition
The space or time something starts, the onset, the commencement, the inception.

Quotes
"Your look of Love renews me, makes me want to fly. Your look of Love it lifts me, I can touch the sky. Now I know what I've been missing has been here all the time and it lets me begin again."
~ Rickie Byars Beckwith

"Learning is the beginning of wealth. Learning is the beginning of health. Learning is the beginning of spirituality. Searching and learning is where the miracle process all begins." ~ Jim Rohn

"Begin to act from your dominion. Declare the Truth by telling yourself that there is nothing to be afraid of, that you no longer entertain any images of fear." ~ Ernest Holmes

Inspirational Message
Expect a miracle every day! Because you are always learning and learning is the beginning of success, the more you learn the more success you achieve. Enjoying the success of wealth, health and/or your spiritual journey is an awesome experience. Delaying or postponing this occurrence is not necessary. Congratulations on commencing this spiritual journey today. At the inception of this journey promise yourself you will take it easy and be open to receiving the gifts of Life.

As you take on this next phase, know that you have choices. The choice to continue on this path is up to you. It is one thing to begin something and it is another to continue it. Just see it as always beginning anew. It is just like today – you have never lived today; so begin this process anew, each day being available to discover and enjoy the way life gives you so much to work with. When you recognize the beginning – there is an opportunity for you to unlock a new idea.

Begin within, each day, believing that the universe is conspiring for your good. Begin within, each day, knowing that there is good in the world and you ought to have it. Begin within, each day, assured that the good that you seek is seeking you.

Spiritual Mind Treatment on Beginning
In the Beginning God! There is One Power, One Presence, One Life – that Life is God. God is all knowing, everywhere present and all powerful. God is Infinite, Indivisible, Absolute, Peace and Love! God is the Creative Intelligence behind everything therefore my life is the Life of God now. As I start anew I speak this prayer as a reminder that I can always begin again.

Beginning now I see that everything comes together for my good. Each moment is a new moment and I enter it with Love, Peace and Joyful expectancy of something amazing. I choose that which is for my highest and best. When I forget I can always begin again with no shame, no blame. My life is filled with all that I need, each time a new beginning. I embrace that there is always newness in each moment. I participate in the flow of life fresh and renewed. I am now open and receptive to all the ways I experience beginnings of every kind.

I am grateful for this Truth. I accept this Truth as my Truth now and give thanks for the richness of beginning. Releasing this word into the Law of God, I joyfully look forward to joy, ease and grace demonstrating in my Life. And so it is!

Affirmation

Today is a new day and my new beginning. On this day I am commencing a beneficial life and a new way of being in the world. I am love. I am kind to all who cross my path today, by speaking an inspiring word, sharing a smile, or being a good listener. Today, I expect a miracle and today I am beginning a successful life of health, wealth and spiritual progress. I am open-minded and willing to begin.

Stillness and Silence, and Journal Writing

Enter a time of stillness and silence. Spend some time free flow writing about Beginning or use the prompt questions on page 18.

Cut out this page and hang it in your bedroom, office, bathroom, kitchen, or anywhere else you will have the opportunity to read it daily. Your Bliss is not lost, just allow it and you'll find it! ♥ Sunshine

Bliss/Joy

Bliss and Joy are natural states of being. Within you there is a wellspring of Bliss and Joy just waiting to give way to a geyser of joy! This month your daily practice will help you uncover your personal treasure chest of Bliss and Joy. Look, you're smiling already!

Definition

A feeling of pleasure or happiness – delight, great pleasure, joyfulness, jubilation, triumph, exultation, rejoicing, happiness, gladness, glee, exhilaration, exuberance, elation, euphoria, bliss, ecstasy, rapture.

Quotes

"To be happy--one must find one's bliss." ~ Gloria Vanderbilt

"Your success and happiness lies in you. Resolve to keep happy, and your joy and you shall form an invincible host against difficulties." ~ Helen Keller

Inspirational Message

Our happiness, joy and bliss exist within us. The idea that something outside of us is responsible for our bliss must be eliminated right now.

In the silence and stillness of your own mind simply ask "what is trying to come forth as me?" What activities am I engaged in when I realize I am happy and joy filled? In what ways is my bliss wanting to express? This is not about following someone else's bliss but discovering, uncovering and embracing your own bliss. Follow the answers that are revealed. Try them out, and allow yourself to fine tune your method of receiving the answers.

Once you find your internal bliss, run and play with it – allow yourself the freedom to indulge in the endless joy that comes from the depths of your soul. You will notice that it was there within you all the time.

Spiritual Mind Treatment Bliss and Joy

I believe in God and only God. God the One Power, One Presence, One Life – That Life is God. God is all knowing, everywhere present and all powerful. God is Joy, Abundance and Beauty! God created everything out of Itself, therefore God is my life now. God is expressing in human form as me. That which is true of God is true of me. I speak the word now from this place of the Joy that God is.

Joy is my natural state. The Joy that God is I am! My life is filled with all joy I need. I am abundant in the bliss that I experience. I am now open and receptive to my unlimited share of bliss. I experience joy in love, finances, career, family, body health and enjoy the bliss from my spiritual practice. I begin within to find my bliss and happiness – it is always right where I am.

With grand appreciation I accept my Truth. My gratitude joyfully expresses within every cell. I give thanks for knowing my Joy and Bliss are within. Releasing this Truth into the Law of God, I joyfully look forward to bliss demonstrating in my Life. And so it is!

Affirmation

I ask, I listen and the answers come from within. I find all the joy and happiness inside of me! I live my Bliss and it shows.

Stillness and Silence, and Journal Writing

Enter a time of stillness and silence. Spend some time free flow writing about Bliss/Joy or use the prompt questions on page 18.

I enjoy the clarity that comes through me.

I am clear and make great decisions in life.

My memory and thoughts are understandable and brilliant.

I am in touch with my highest good.

Clarity

Rev. Sunshine Daye

Cut out this page and hang it in your bedroom, office, bathroom, kitchen, or anywhere else you will have the opportunity to read it daily. Crazy about your beauty ~ Sunshine ♥

Clarity

Clarity provides the opportunity to enjoy life without ambiguity and haziness. This month, your daily practice is designed to deepen your connection with your inner guidance. Clarity is born when you release your busy thoughts, and allow yourself to hear the quiet voice within.

Definition
Clearness, brightness, splendor, freedom from obstruction, being clear, free from uncertainty, free from doubt.

Quotes
"For me the greatest beauty always lies in the greatest clarity." ~ Gotthold Ephraim Lessing

"People who lack the clarity, courage, or determination to follow their own dreams often find ways to discourage yours. Live your Truth and don't ever stop!" ~ Steve Maraboli

Inspirational Message
Expect the miracle of clarity every day! Becoming clear takes a little inside work. However, consider it work *and* play! Because of the work you can truly enjoy the opportunities to play. When folks have clarity they can see the beauty beyond any obstacles that may seem in the way.

If you are the captain of your ship traveling along the sea, a clear day is always better than a day with low-lying clouds. Having clarity allows you the opportunity to navigate your life in the direction that best suits you and fulfills your life's mission. You can achieve clarity around career, love relationships, friendships, and everyday occurrences when you use the daily practice of going within and asking questions. You have within you an internal navigation system that, when activated, can direct you and guide you to that which is your highest good at any given moment.

When you ask others what you should do with your life, your relationships, or your problems, you are saying in effect *I am not the captain of my ship*. Make it your daily practice to set aside some time of stillness and silence, asking your higher self for the clarity necessary to proceed throughout the day. Allow yourself to be guided throughout the day, surrender to clarity and go within for the right decisions. You will have the clarity to know what is best.

Begin within, each day, believing that the universe is conspiring for your good. Begin within, each day, knowing that there is good in the world and you ought to have it.

Spiritual Mind Treatment on Clarity
There is a Divine Life that has created all life and everything is made from this Source. I call it Love, Life, I call it God. The more I awaken to this Truth, I am clear that God is All – therefore my life is the life of God. I am one with this Power and Presence. In God there is no confusion, no ambiguity only clarity. I speak the word from this place of Clarity.

The clarity that God is I am. I accept the clarity that is already present within me. I listen and allow the Divine Presence in and as me to orchestrate my life. I am in accordance with the Divine Law of clarity and I am focused, allowing my insight and foresight to expresses as me in every area of my life. I experience clarity in my mental body, my emotional body and my physical body. The Indwelling Presence operates clearly as my life and I move in accordance with this law of right action. Everything is coming together for my good.

I give thanks for knowing of this Truth and especially for the manifestation of this word now. With ease and grand appreciation I accept clarity. My gratitude overflows.

Releasing this Truth into the Law of God, I joyfully look forward to my demonstrations.

And so it is!

Affirmation

I enjoy the clarity that comes through me. I am clear and make great decisions in life. My memory and thoughts are brilliant and understandable. I am in touch with my highest good.

Stillness and Silence, and Journal Writing

Enter a time of stillness and silence. Spend some time free flow writing about Bliss/Joy or use the prompt questions on page 18.

Connectedness

I am one with every life
and all life is one with me.
God is living as me now.
I am connected with everyone.
I am connected with nature.
My life thrives as I know my connectedness.

Rev. Sunshine Daye

Cut out this page and hang it in your bedroom, office, bathroom, kitchen, or anywhere else you will have the opportunity to read it daily. I can't wait to see the color of your wings! ♥ Sunshine

Connectedness

Feeling disconnected is not pleasant. Deepen your awareness that we are all connected and experience the sense of community, friendship, love and connection. We are all connected, even when in the natural, physical realm it may not seem so. When you use Connectedness as your source of focus for this month there is no limit to your joy!

Definition
A state of being linked. Bring together or in contact so that a real or notional link is established, Join together so as to provide access and communication.

Quotes
"I work really hard at trying to see the big picture and not getting stuck in ego. I believe we're all put on this planet for a purpose, and we all have a different purpose... When you connect with that love and that compassion, that's when everything unfolds." ~ Ellen DeGeneres

"I used to think that I needed somebody – all I needed was my connection with God."
~ Michael and Rickie Byars Beckwith

Inspirational Message
We are all connected. We are all one. Science tells us that we are made of the same stuff the stars are made of. As soon as we accept the fact that we are part of the universal mind, and that which is true about Life is true about us, we begin to feel our connection with and our connectedness with all things. We experience connectedness to the degree that we accept it. When we accept our connectedness, our Oneness with all life, and the Wholeness that we are, we begin to live life from the perspective that everything is working in conjunction with all things. This experience is symphonic, synergistic, and purposeful; the belief in separation has always been an illusion.

It is through dedicated prayer, meditation, sacred service and giving that one begins to see and feel the connectedness of Life. Many people join groups, particularly social media groups and support groups to feel connected; it is our natural instinct to do so. Even a loner recognizes that she or he is connected with all of life. When you feel or think that you are alone, remember that this really means al-one.

Begin within, each day recognizing your oneness. See it with others, see it with pets or animals, plant life, and recognize your connectedness with the foods you eat, the water you drink and the clothes you wear. Remember there were many hands involved in getting you the foods you eat, the clothes you wear, the products in your home, and the roads you walk or drive on. We are connected. See all things as being intimately connected to you.

Spiritual Mind Treatment on Connectedness
In the moment I stop to recognize God. God is the One Power, One Presence, and One Life that has created all things. This creative Intelligence produces life from itself, therefore all life contains the essence of God. I am one with this Essence – It is who I am and it expresses fully as me in this and every moment. I recognize God as Love, Intelligence, Harmony, Peace and Unity. I treat my mind with the knowing that God is my life now. I speak the word for myself from this place in consciousness.

The connectedness that God is I am. The thoughts I think are the thoughts of the I Am presence because we are connected. I enjoy the feeling of unity with all life and I choose opportunities that encourage cooperation, collaboration and community. When I am aware that I am Love and Compassion, everything unfolds for my highest good. I share my gifts and talents knowing that this is an out picturing of connection in action. I benefit greatly and the world benefits greatly from this simple knowing that connectedness is nature. I appreciate our oneness. I participate in the flow of life. I am now open and receptive to my unlimited sense of connection.

I give thanks for the Truth of my Oneness in God and my connection to all life. With ease and grand appreciation, I accept my good. Releasing this Truth into the Law of God, I joyfully look forward to it demonstrating in my Life. And so it is!

Affirmation

I am one with every life and all life is one with me. God is living as me now. I am connected with everyone. I am connected with nature. My life thrives as I know my connectedness.

Stillness and Silence, and Journal Writing

Enter a time of stillness and silence. Spend some time free flow writing about Bliss/Joy or use the prompt questions on page 18.

FAITH

My faith is strong.

I use faith to build
my beautiful experience and life!

Rev. Sunshine Daye

Cut out this page and hang it in your bedroom, office, bathroom, kitchen, or anywhere else you will have the opportunity to read it daily. Keep the Faith! ♥ Sunshine

Faith

Everyone has some degree of faith - even when it does not seem so. When you use Faith as your carrot this month you will discover an increase in personal power. Remember they key is engaging in your daily practice.

Definition
Complete trust or confidence in someone or something without proof.

Quotes
"Be faithful in small things because it is in them that your strength lies." ~ Mother Teresa

"Really fear is nothing more than misplaced faith – faith in a power opposed to good."
~ Ernest Holmes

Inspirational Message
These days we use the word faith to relay a deep trust in a process, a person, or thing. I have faith that if I am in a dark room and I get up to turn on the switch that the light will turn on. True enough I have seen this happen thousands of times before but what makes me think that it's going to happen this time? It is the trust! Faith is the energetic that propels me forward in action.

In what do you trust? Are you the person who must see it to believe it? Or are you the one who is so in tune with life that you know there is a flow, an energetic and operation at all times that is conspiring for your highest good?

The consciousness of faith requires that you examine your beliefs in order to uncover any false notions, ideas, attitudes and ways of life that are hindering your success. Since faith is the force and energetic that propels you forward in trusting and knowing, then it stands to reason you want to be propelled in a direction that is towards your wholeness, joy and bounty.

Look at your behavior. Do you react or respond? Does your behavior prove you are living from shame, doubt, doom and gloom or from delight, trust, joy and expectancy? The proof is in the pudding. Clearly, when we are "faithful in small things" we are propelled to delight and trust in joyful expectation that the outcome will be for our good, rather than being propelled by fear to act in selfish, self-centered, and egotistical ways. The small victories prepare us for the big ones.

Begin within, each day, living faithfully with delight, trust, joy and expectancy. Recognize your beliefs in "life limiting" ideas and get rid of them by replacing "life limiting" with "life affirming" and "life enhancing" characteristics, like, abundance, beauty, creativity, wholeness, peace, joy and harmony. Then recognize them all surrounding you and living within you. Begin within, each day, strongly believing you live in a beautiful world.

Spiritual Mind Treatment on Faith
I take a mindful pause to recognize the One Power, One Presence, and One Life that is God. God! Omnipresent, Omniscient and Omnipotent. I know God to be Absolute Creativity, Peace and Love! As God has created everything from Itself, I am steeped in the knowing that my life is that Life of God, expressing magnificently in human form as me and as all things seen and unseen. Therefore that which is true of God is true of me because this One Life is expressing in many forms. As I know this about God and myself I also know this same Truth about all life! I speak the word regarding faith in my life.

The faith of God is the faith of my life. I experience and express faith in perfect and divine ways. It is easy and effortless to know that my faith carries me through each life situation. The wisdom of God that is present right where I am guides me every step of the way. Faith is expressed in all my affairs. I am in complete harmony with the faith that I am.

I give thanks for the realization of this word spoken and for its perfect out-picturing in my life. I am grateful to know this Truth. Releasing this Truth into the Law of God, I joyfully look forward its demonstration in my Life. And so it is!

Affirmation
My faith is strong. I use faith to build my beautiful experience and life!

Stillness and Silence, and Journal Writing
Enter a time of stillness and silence. Spend some time free flow writing about Bliss/Joy or use the prompt questions on page 18.

Imagine

All my good is already given, and I joyfully accept it now!
I use my imagination to recognize my wholeness
and I see and I believe I am whole now.
Today, I imagine peace with my mind's eye,
and see it with my physical eye.
I allow my sensations to carry me through to success.

Rev. Sunshine Daye

Cut out this page and hang it in your bedroom, office, bathroom, kitchen, or anywhere else you will have the opportunity to read it daily. Imagine that! ♥ Sunshine

Imagine

What are you willing to imagine? When you use Imagine, as your gift for this month you will value and appreciate the ability to mentally conceive. This month, your daily practice expands upon your initial powers of imagination.

Definition
Form a mental image, believe in something real or unreal.

Quotes
"Winners, I am convinced, imagine their dreams first. They want it with all their hearts and expect it to come true. There is, I believe, no other way to live." ~ Joe Montana

"My imagination is a monastery, and I am its monk." ~ John Keats

Inspirational Message
Make a mental picture of it all. This is all about imaging it and embodying the imagery to such a degree that when we are ready - it is given, and we accept it. Remember that you are dealing with Divine Intelligence and a power that simply says "Yes!"

When you see yourself as poor, sick, and broken, what out-pictures is the same. Therefore it serves you to be as vivid with your imagination as possible. By saying yes and envisioning your life as abundant, healthy and joyous you not only prove the law of reflection and the law of attraction with the demonstration but you also participate in giving the greatest gift to the world. There is a power for good and you can use it. Yes!

Imagine living from a calm, peaceful, confident, loving, harmonious place on a regular basis. This is not some pie-in-the-sky thinking, rather, it is a reality that directly results from knowing your Truth. This is why so many folks in Alcoholics Anonymous , all over the world, have been successful in living amazing lives. The deep practice of the 11th step, seeking to improve conscious contact with God through prayer and meditation, has provided so many the feeling of being happy, joyous and free!

Spiritual Mind Treatment on Imagine
The Power, Presence and Life that has created all things – I recognize as God. God is all knowing, everywhere present and all powerful. God is Creative Intelligence, Indivisible, Absolute, Beauty, Peace and Love! God created everything out Itself therefore that life is my life now. God is expressing in human form as me. That which is true of God is true of me. My life is the life of God.

As I know this about God and myself I also know this same Truth about all life! I speak this word now with the same authority as the one that has created me.

I now accept that my mind creates from Infinite Intelligence. My imagination is keen and creativity flows from me easily and effortlessly. The ideas, thoughts and intuitive notions that I entertain are beautiful, perfect and they generate gifts to humanity in infinite ways. I allow myself the pleasure, opportunity and gift of imagination, knowing that it serves a high calling.

My imagination serves me well. The imagination of God is my imagination now! With ease and grand appreciation I accept my imagination. My gratitude joyfully expresses internally and externally. I give thanks for the knowing of this Truth. I now release this prayer into the Law of God. I joyfully look forward to all the ways my imagination demonstrates in my Life.

And so it is!

Affirmation

All my good is already given and I joyfully accept it now! I use my imagination to recognize my wholeness and I see and I believe I am whole now. Today, I imagine peace with my mind's eye and see it with my physical eye. I allow my sensations to carry me through to success.

Stillness and Silence, and Journal Writing

Enter a time of stillness and silence. Spend some time free flow writing about Bliss/Joy or use the prompt questions on page 18.

Cut out this page and hang it in your bedroom, office, bathroom, kitchen, or anywhere else you will have the opportunity to read it daily. Let Peace begin with us! ♥ Sunshine

Peace

When peace becomes the place you live from, life becomes peace-filled. As you use Peace as your inspiration for this month you will grow in understanding of just how much peace actually exists within you. Your daily practice this month magnifies peace in all areas of life.

Definition
Tranquility, freedom from disturbance, harmony, non-violence.

Quotes
"When the power of love overcomes the love of power the world will know peace." ~ Jimi Hendrix

"Peace is not the absence of chaos or conflict, but rather finding yourself in the midst of that chaos and remaining calm in your heart." ~ John Mroz

Inspirational Message
Sometimes peace eludes us because we can get so caught up in the day to day activity or chaos of life. The practices of meditation, yoga, prayer and service are simple tools we can use to remind us of our inner peace. You must recognize that you have the power to accept and create peace in your own life. Say to yourself, "It is truly up to me."

You may contribute to a peaceful situation in the life of another – however only you can stop the mental chatter in your own head and choose to live a drama-free life. "It is truly up to me."

Sy Miller and Jill Jackson wrote the song "Let There Be Peace on Earth." *Let there be peace on earth, and let it begin with me*. This song always reminds me that I am in charge of my interior landscape, and I can choose peace in any situation. Ever wonder if it's really that easy? You can start with having a calm heart. There is a solution - find your solution! If the secret to living a peace-filled life is as simple as having a calm heart, then try it!

Begin within – start today living with a calm heart. Think serene thoughts that cause your heart calmness and peace. Walk, talk and behave in a tranquil way so your heart and life can move in the peaceful direction of your desire. Envision a peaceful life for yourself and others.

Being at peace doesn't mean that you will never face chaos or strife again, but rather when those times arise you will deal with them in a calm, serene and peaceful fashion. Ah yes! Peace is mine.

Spiritual Mind Treatment on Peace
No Power exists outside of the One Power, One Presence, and One Life that is God. God - all knowing, everywhere present and all powerful. God is Infinite, Absolute, Peace and Love! I am one with this Power and Presence. As I know this about God and myself I also know this same Truth about all life! As the direct creation of God, I speak this word now from a place of power, knowing this prayer is already answered and is a Law unto itself. I now speak my word into brilliant manifestation.

My thoughts are thoughts of peace. I experience peace of mind. I choose peace in each situation and I experience peace in my body and spirit. My surroundings are peace-filled! That which is for my highest and best is centered in amity. I am a wonderful steward of my life, demonstrating peaceful use of it. I peaceful share my gifts and talents. Plenty flows to me and through me as I participate in the calm flow of life. I am now open and receptive to my unlimited tranquility. I display grand appreciation for all the harmony in my life. The Peace of God is my peace now!

My gratitude is immense as I joyfully express thanks for the knowing of Peace as my life and the continual unfoldment of my peaceful life.

Releasing this Truth into the Law of God, I look forward to more peace demonstrating in my Life.

And so it is!

Affirmation

My heart is serene. My life is filled with peace. I am the peace that I seek. All is well. I am the center of peace and peace is at the center of me.

Stillness and Silence, and Journal Writing

Enter a time of stillness and silence. Spend some time free flow writing about Bliss/Joy or use the prompt questions on page 18.

Purpose

I live a life of purpose and I am purpose driven!

Rev. Sunshine Daye

Cut out this page and hang it in your bedroom, office, bathroom, kitchen, or anywhere else you will have the opportunity to read it daily. Your joy IS your purpose! ♥ Sunshine

Purpose

Experience the joy of purpose in your life! As you focus on Purpose this month, be gentle with yourself and be committed to the daily practice.

Definition
The reason for which something is created, the reason for which something exists, the reason for which something is done, motivation, the feeling of being driven.

Quotes
"Our prime purpose in life is to help others. And if you can't help them, at least don't hurt them."
~ His Holiness Dali Lama

"Learn to get in touch with the silence within yourself and know that everything in life has a purpose. There are no mistakes, no coincidences, all events are blessings given to us to learn from."
~ Elisabeth Kubler Ross

"When you live your life with purpose and when you are in touch with your life's purpose you allow yourself to be…Thus becoming a HEARTist." ~ Amoke Carolyn Warren and Sunshine Daye

Inspirational Message
How many times have you wondered, "Why am I here and what is my purpose?" Of course these are questions that you may have asked yourself a million times! You exist so that Life may have a one-of-a-kind expression as you. You and I are the way God expresses Itself on the planet. So what is your purpose? Live, beloved, live! When you can just be yourself, God is free to express Itself, in any way that you choose! This is great news!

Enjoy yourself, be happy, and get excited about the marvelous life that awaits you! Still don't know your purpose? Imagine yourself living with no money concerns, traveling, talking to people, cooking, doing whatever is a passion for you. Find your personal purpose – write a list of what you do for fun, and things you enjoy doing. Next make a list of people you admire and why you admire them. Then make a list of things that seem to come easily and naturally to you. This list may include things like your ability to nurture, having an eye for detail, drawing or being playful and humorous. Anything that brings you pleasure can go on the lists! Each day look at the three lists and do something from each list for at least 10 minutes. Have fun, tell someone how you feel about them and do something that comes naturally to you. Do it even if fear pops up – just move through it. Your purpose will make itself known to you!

Spiritual Mind Treatment on Purpose
I believe in God and nothing else. God - the One Power, One Presence, One Life, which is omniscient, omnipresent and omnipotent! God is Creative Intelligence, Abundance, Beauty, Peace and Love! My life is the life of God – therefore it is true of me. As I know this about God and myself I also know this same Truth about all life! The word that I speak now is from the place of Oneness.

My life has a purpose and is on purpose. My purpose becomes clear to me in each and every situation. I surrender gracefully to my purpose knowing that as I surrender, all things come together for my good. My thoughts are purposeful and mindful. I purposefully choose that which is for the highest and best for all involved. My life is filled with purpose.

I use my purpose to benefit life. Because I live on purpose, plenty flows to me and through me as I participate in the flow of life. The purpose of God is my purpose.

I give thanks for the clear knowing of my purpose. My gratitude joyfully expresses within me as I am grateful for the knowing of this Truth and the manifestation it.

Releasing this Truth into the Law of God, I joyfully look forward my purpose demonstrating in my Life. And so it is!

Affirmation
I live a life of purpose and I am purpose driven!

Stillness and Silence, and Journal Writing
Enter a time of stillness and silence. Spend some time free flow writing about Bliss/Joy or use the prompt questions on page 18.

Thankfulness

I am acquainted with the value and benefits I receive,
by means of Life and my own actions.
I am thankful for all the gifts bestowed upon me.
In a consciousness of gratitude I freely redistribute my good to life.
I see the beauty in others.
I enjoy my attitude of gratitude and it shows!

Rev. Sunshine Daye

Cut out this page and hang it in your bedroom, office, bathroom, kitchen, or anywhere else you will have the opportunity to read it daily. I am thankful for YOU! ♥ Sunshine

Thankfulness

Thankfulness is a wonderful way of being. As you use Thankfulness as your motivation this month you will cultivate the art of thankfulness. Your daily practice this month magnifies the gifts you receive.

Definition
Conscious of benefit received, aware and appreciative of, the expression of gratitude, to God, via prayer.

Quotes
"The enlightened give thanks for what most people take for granted." ~ Rev. Michael Beckwith

"Be thankful for what you have; you'll end up having more. If you concentrate on what you don't have, you will never, ever have enough." ~ Oprah Winfrey

Inspirational Message
What are the subtle differences between thankfulness, gratitude and appreciation? The feeling tone of appreciating is a conscious recognition that there is value being added to my life, and that in each moment of recognition my gratitude is increased. The action I take to express gratitude is thankfulness.

The consciousness of thankfulness is developed and incorporated when you mindfully begin to count the value, gifts and blessings that have been added to your life by no direct means of your own efforts. When you begin to add up the gifts of the sun, trees, moon, atmosphere and all the life-affirming systems we have in place, there will be an inner sense of thankfulness that wells up, in recognition of the simple fact that the world - in fact the entire universe - is conspiring for our good. Through no conscious effort your heart beats, your lungs inhale and exhale, your organs function in your body's system, and everything runs 24/7! We can to become thankful that we don't have to remember to activate our organs, our heart or lungs in order to continue this amazing life.

Begin within, each day, thankful for all the value that is added to you and all the value that you add to others. Recognize your beauty and then recognize the beauty that surrounds you. Begin within, each day, believing you live in a beautiful world.

Spiritual Mind Treatment on Thankfulness
There is One Power, One Presence, One Life – That Life is God. God is all knowing, everywhere present and all-powerful. God is Abundance, Infinite, Indivisible, Absolute, Beauty, Peace and Love! God created everything out of Itself, therefore that life is my life now. God is expressing in human form as me. That which is true of God is true of me since my life is the life of God in human form. This One Life is What I Am! As I know this about God and myself, I also know this same Truth about all life!

As I focus on being thankful, I open to a greater sense of joy, peace and prosperity. I am now receptive to noticing the gifts of life and experiencing gratitude on a deeper level. Gratitude is my natural state and I accept it now. The thoughts I think are the thoughts of the I Am presence that is my Life. I choose that which is for my highest and best and I give thanks for this inner guidance. My life is filled with all that I need and for this I give thanks. I give freely and share my gifts and talents. With ease and grand appreciation I accept my part of the Universal Good. My gratitude joyfully expresses within every cell. I give thanks for the knowing of this Truth.

Releasing this Truth into the Law of God, I joyfully look forward to a multitude of demonstrations in my Life.

And so it is!

Affirmation

I am acquainted with the value and benefits I receive by means of Life and my own actions. I am thankful for all the gifts bestowed upon me. In a consciousness of gratitude I freely redistribute my good to life. I see the beauty in others. I enjoy my attitude of gratitude and it shows!

Stillness and Silence, and Journal Writing

Enter a time of stillness and silence. Spend some time free flow writing about Bliss/Joy or use the prompt questions on page 18.

Cut out this page and hang it in your bedroom, office, bathroom, kitchen, or anywhere else you will have the opportunity to read it daily. Feel your 'whole-iness'... ♥ Sunshine

Wholeness

You are whole even when it does not seem so. When you place your attention on Wholeness this month you will develop a strong sense of how your life is filled with wholeness. This month, your daily practice broadens upon your current concept of what wholeness is.

Definition
Containing all components; complete, not divided or disjoined; in one unit, constituting the full amount, extent, or duration.

Quotes
"To be great, be whole; Exclude nothing, exaggerate nothing that is not you. Be whole in everything. Put all you are into the smallest thing you do. So, in each lake, the moon shines with splendor because it blooms up above." ~ Fernando Pessoa

"We need to see, and agree that what we seek already lives within us, and we within it. Now we know our one great task: watch for whatever promises us freedom, and then quietly, consciously refuse to see ourselves through the eyes of what we know is incomplete. Then we live wholeness itself, instead of spending our lives looking for it." ~ Guy Finley

Inspirational Message
Behold, you are whole. Be whole!! You can't help but be whole right now. Even when you do not feel whole, it cannot take an inch off of the wholeness that you are! Your experience may be different but your essence is wholeness.

When you allow your true essence to emerge from within you, your experiences will match your true essence. As long as you fight your true essence, with your mistaken thoughts, misperceptions and false beliefs, you are bound to have feelings of separation from your essence.

Begin within! Recognize and reunite daily with your true identity. Celebrate your wholeness and all the ways you show up. Let go of who you think you are and get in touch with who you really are.

Spiritual Mind Treatment on Wholeness
I believe in God and nothing else. The whole, loving Presence that is God has created everything, therefore my life is that Life that God is. As I know this about God and myself I also know this same Truth about all life! The Oneness in which I live, breathe and have my being-ness is God. I anchor this in my consciousness, now speaking the word for and about the wholeness that I am.

The wholeness that God is I am. I accept the wholeness of my body temple, of my affairs and I now accept the whole of my emotional and spiritual bodies. The thoughts I think are the thought of the I Am presence that is my wholeness. I choose that which is for my highest and best good. I am wonderfully whole, demonstrating my wholeness in every aspect of my life. My life is filled with joy. I am abundant. I give freely of my gifts and talents from my wholeness knowing that I cannot be depleted.

I am thankful to know this Truth about the wholeness that I am. My gratitude joyfully expresses in many ways.

Releasing this Truth into the Law of God, I joyfully look forward to wholeness demonstrating as my Life. And so it is!

Affirmation
In this very moment I am whole. My wholeness shows up in so many amazing ways. I enjoy my physical, emotional, mental and spiritual wholeness now.

Stillness and Silence, and Journal Writing
Enter a time of stillness and silence. Spend some time free flow writing about Bliss/Joy or use the prompt questions on page 18.

Rev. Sunshine Daye

Cut out this page and hang it in your bedroom, office, bathroom, kitchen, or anywhere else you will have the opportunity to read it daily. All your worth is already within you. ♥ Sunshine

Worthiness

Experience worthiness beyond what you currently know. When you use Worthiness as your impetus this month you will develop a strong sense of your worth. To experience it, be with it daily.

Definition
Having merit or value; useful or valuable, honorable, admirable and deserving.

Quotes
"The most splendid achievement of all is the constant striving to surpass yourself and to be worthy of your own approval." ~ Denis Waitley

"It is a full time job being honest one moment at a time, remembering to love, to honor, to respect. It is a practice, a discipline worthy of every moment." ~ Jasmine Guy

Inspirational Message
What do you long for? I know what I long for. When I go deep within I see the Truth is there. Wow! It's life in me, in you and everywhere!

You are worthy of abundance, beauty, and joy. Your body temple is healthy and well. Your life is filled with harmony, wisdom, creativity, and of all these things you are worthy.

Spiritual Mind Treatment on Worth
I believe in God and nothing else; the One Life, everywhere present, all knowing, all powerful, creative Intelligence that has created me out of itself. This life that is God is my life now, therefore I now make known my desires and accept them as manifest facts of my life. That which God is – is present in my life and accessible to me by speaking my word and by being at one with Love, Joy, Peace, Clarity, Abundance and Wholeness. As I know this about God and myself I also know this same Truth about all life! This word I speak now is a Law unto itself being made fulfilled even now!

I am now clear in my heart and mind that the worthiness that I desire is put into motion and produces the results of a deep inner knowing of my worth. I experience a sense of worthiness because I am steeped in the knowing that my life is the life of God. Because there is nothing that separates my life from the One Life, then the sense of worthiness I desire comes naturally, as I recognize that my life is neither less than or greater than any life.

I give thanks for this Truth and its manifestation as my life. The Law knows exactly how to manifest my sense of worth, so I release my word into this Presence now. I let go of any thoughts of concern, lack or limitation, and I embrace and enjoy the manifestation of Worth. For this I give grateful thanks.

And so it is!

Affirmation
I am worthy of abundance and infinite possibility. Life constantly shows me that I am worthy of the air I breathe, the trees, love, joy, fun, and all that I am willing to accept.

Stillness and Silence, and Journal Writing
Enter a time of stillness and silence. Spend some time free flow writing about Bliss/Joy or use the prompt questions on page 18.

Acknowledgements

I am grateful to us! Sunny Daye, I am grateful for the love and support we provide one another and I'm in amazement at the depth of your love for me. Thankfulness overflows for my parents, Ana and Anthony Silva, for raising me to know that only Love matters. Family and Friends, I am thankful for your support to print this book and for the many ways we show up in each other's lives, it is priceless.

Caitlin Crest of Zephyr Graphics fills my heart with gratitude and awe for the creativity that flows through her onto the pages of this book.

I am in deep appreciation for the editing skills of my friends Rev. Dr. Judy Mattivi Morely, Lori Gertz and Dr. Louise Tallen RScP, you made my sentiments readable.

Major thanks to Shauna McNamara for the cover design.

I have an immense sense of gratitude for my beloved brother and mentor, Michael Bernard Beckwith D.D., Founder and Spiritual Director, Agape International Spiritual Center; his "Yes" to Spirit gave me permission to say "Yes!" too.

Joy fills me with gratitude for the expanded awareness of the energy field of Love!

Thank you for reading this book!

Please receive your free gift by logging onto sunshinedaye.com/begin-within-offer.

Visit www.SunshineDaye.com
to enjoy more of Sunshine's
inspirational thoughts, videos and products.

Closing Thoughts

Well done beloved and cheers on journeying into this essential spiritual inner work. As you know, it takes effort, energy and an aspiration to reveal the Indwelling Magnificence that is your birthright. Now this is way of life for you! I hope you feel confident, loved, courageous and highly benefitted from new level of understanding and growth.

You are amazing!

You have everything within to live a fulfilling life. The answers are truly within you and you can trust the flow of Life to be for your highest good.

You have revealed a greater truth!

Remember to care for yourself and others. Engage in activities that feed and nourish your soul. Give and get plenty of hugs, enjoy human connections, and see God in everyone and every situation. Continue your daily spiritual practices and have fun!

Remember, it doesn't end here – you can use this book to go beyond where you are now. Yes, you can enhance your existing sense of Worthiness, Love, Bliss, etc., just turn to that page, write the date on top and Begin Within!

Love always rules,

Sunshine Daye

More About Rev. Sunshine Daye

Rev. Sunshine is an ordained minister through The Centers for Spiritual Living. She received her Master's degree and studied at Holmes Institute under the guidance of Michael Bernard Beckwith, D.D., Founder and Spiritual Director, Agape International Spiritual Center.

Rev. Sunshine is a gifted speaker who transforms lives and helps people live their genuine life through spiritual practice. Sunshine grew up in a diverse part of the Bronx where Puerto Ricans, Blacks, Whites, Jews, drug and numbers runners, and gangsters co-existed. From a young age Sunshine learned to appreciate each individual's humanness and the value of each life.

Rev. Sunshine's has always been a spiritual seeker. As a child she studied Catholicism and then was a practicing member of the Jehovah's Witnesses for many years. In addition, Rev. Sunshine has studied Buddhism and other Eastern traditions.

Rev. Sunshine's depth and breadth of spiritual study and life experience gives her a unique ability to meet people where they are and to appreciate the beauty in everyone, everywhere.

In 2009 Rev. Sunshine was awarded the Gene Lentzner Human Relations Awards from the California Conference for Equality and Justice, and was honored by Long Beach Pride as the Female Community Grand Marshal.

When you experience her energy and the joy that radiates from her you will understand why Rev. Sunshine's motto is:

"By means of your spiritual practice you live your Genuine Life."

More thoughts

More jots

More :)

CPSIA information can be obtained at www.ICGtesting.com
Printed in the USA
BVIW12n1109110416
443772BV00006B/17